THE OLDEST GIANT WINE BARREL

A SUPERLATIVE AT HOHENTÜBINGEN CASTLE

D1666580

Brief Monographs by MUT
Published by Ernst Seidl and Michael La Corte

Volume 14

Edgar Bierende

The Oldest Giant Wine Barrel

A SUPERLATIVE AT HOHENTÜBINGEN CASTLE

For Christiane
and my daughters Helene and Pauline

CONTENT

Fig. 1   Tübingen Giant Barrel

INTRODUCTION

Numerous anecdotes, stories and legends surround Hohentübingen Castle. One of them is about the Tübingen Giant Barrel, which was once supposedly filled with wine —a controversial presumption. Its non-public and virtually invisible placement and sheer size have always captured people's imaginations. The Giant Barrel is about 6.80 m long and about 4.70 m high. Twenty wooden segmental rings, secured with forged iron bands, span 78 beam-like barrel staves. The whole barrel rests on massive barrel-bearing beams, which provide the construction with additional support and height. This wooden colossus was probably used as a wine reservoir, even if only at the very beginning, and is still considered a cultural and historical highlight and tourist attraction today.

Many visitors still come today to see the gigantic barrel with their own eyes. The size, the location in the cellar of the castle and its age fascinate people. Additionally, on the interior of the barrel, numerous graffiti and scratchings from four centuries (Fig. 2) by visitors and wine-soppy revellers who immortalised themselves on the historic monument with their names and a date can be found. According to many older Tübingen citizens, student parties are said to have taken place around and in the barrel again and again until well into the middle of the twentieth century, which

Fig. 2   Chalk drawings in the Giant Barrel

explains many of the chalk drawings. Today the Giant Barrel is a touristic curiosity with a wide range of echoes in literature and art, and has been mentioned, described and depicted again and again in various contexts.

A literary prelude of a special kind is the first mention of the "large barrel at Tübingen Castle"[1] in Johann Fischart's (ca. 1548–1590; Fig. 3) famous *Geschichtklitterung* as early as 1575. Fischart, who presumably studied for a while in the Faculty of Arts in Tübingen[2], describes the Tübingen Barrel in his fantastically grotesque and witty satirical tale about the adventures and the drinking bouts of the giant Gargantua. His book is based on the work *Gargantua und Pantagruel* (1532; Fig. 4), written by the French author François Rabelais (1494–1553), which, early on, caused a sensation and was well received on many levels. For example, Richard Breton (1524–1571; Fig. 5) printed a series of 120 woodcuts by François Desprez (1525–1580) in Paris.[3] Fischart enriched the celebrated work of Rabelais with many verbal reinterpretations, fresh acrobatic twists and novel associative word cascades. Among them are many allusions to local traditions and academic customs and practices. In the midst of this exuberant humanistic erudition between realistic and fantastic descriptions and in the witty-ironic jumble of voices of the Giant-Reveller, the Tübingen Giant Barrel emerged from the darkness of the castle cellar into the light of a reading public. In this manner, a new perspective on the Tübingen Giant Barrel was released and would become trendsetting in the sense of the cheerful-folkloric, rabelaisian and fischartian joke. Many other descriptions and mentions in literature followed: in books about the history of the city of Tübingen,[4] in writings about the

| Fig. 3 | Christoph Murer: Portrait of Johann Fischart, 1607 | Fig. 4 | Title page, in: François Rabelais: Les Grandes |

regional history[5] and in a description[6] of Württemberg, in publications about the craft of coopers,[7] and, more recently, on postcards, in travel literature[8] and art history[9]. All this speaks not only for the former fame of the Giant Barrel, but also for its widespread and popular reception. It is all the more regrettable that it has fallen into oblivion nowadays. There are two reasons for the disappearance of the Giant Barrel out of the public focus—one animal and one human. Since the mid-1970s, a colony of mouse-eared bats has been living in the vaulted cellar. As bats and their habitats are strictly protected and must not be disturbed, the barrel has not been accessible to the public since 1994. However, since January 2018, the Giant Barrel in the cellar

of the castle of Tübingen is once again open to the public. Visitors are allowed only in small groups at specific times in order to protect the bats and their habitat. The second reason is obvious to everyone who has stood in front of the barrel: it is empty; and where there is no more wine, it becomes quiet and lonely. The ancient poet Horace described a similar experience in one of his famous odes: "Diffugiunt cadis cum faece siccatis amici."[10]—"When the barrel is empty, friends wipe their mouths and leave."[11]

THE AGE OF THE BARREL

A text is written on the front of the barrel, but it has faded over the centuries (Fig. 6). Last traces show that names and dates were written in the upper area. One date is written at the top. Three of the four numbers in the top line are readable: 15[...]3. Below that a division into three columns and two registers is discernible. A year can be deciphered, which is repeatedly mentioned in six places: "1563". This was a cold and rainy year with poor harvests and high inflation. Beneath the year 1563, there are two individual letters in two lines and a name below them. Only in the lowest register can two names still be deciphered: "Oich | Cammerer" and "Wedell". At the top, the blurred name "Bran[denb]urg" can be surmised.[12]

In 1563, the office of the court sexton[13] at Hohentübingen Castle was filled again. To which historical event the recurring year 1563 and the seven names refer, or in other words, which specific events the inscription is supposed to evoke, can no longer be deduced from preserved sources. Thus, the reason for the inscription remains unknown. It's certain that the Giant Barrel must have been built before this date.

On several old photos and postcards (Fig. 7) of the Tübingen Giant Barrel a wooden plaque with a poem, probably dated around 1900, is visible on the barrel. This wooden plaque

Fig. 6   Tübingen Giant Barrel with inscription from 1563

Fig. 7   Barrel with poem on wooden plaque, around 1930

briefly answered the visitor's most important questions: Who was the client? When was it made? How big is the Giant Barrel and what is it made of?

The wooden plaque with the poem is lost. A metal plate was attached to the barrel in its place, on which the same text is written. It probably dates back to the 1930s (Fig. 8) and stands nowadays at the bottom next to the Giant Barrel:

> "I am known as the great book,
> So named by Duke Ulrich.
> I was built in 1546,
> From 90 oaks as you can see.
> I was twice filled with wine,
> I accommodate 286 buckets."

Due to previously unpublished source material, it is now possible to check the data and information in the poem and enrich it with further details and facts. It is certain—as all records agree—that Duke Ulrich of Württemberg (1487–1550; Fig. 9) commissioned the Giant Barrel of Tübingen. Ulrich was an extremely dazzling character who polarised in more than one way. He ruled Württemberg for a very long time, from 1498 until 1550, albeit with a 15-year-long interruption due to his expulsion from the state.

After his return as sovereign prince, Ulrich enforced the Reformation. One centre of his reign lay in Tübingen where he greatly expanded the local castle into Hohentübingen Castle. It was one of a total of seven castles he had expanded into state strongholds. They include, among others: Hohenneuffen, Hohentwiel, Hohenurach and Hohenasperg. Ulrich repeatedly lived at Hohentübingen for long periods of

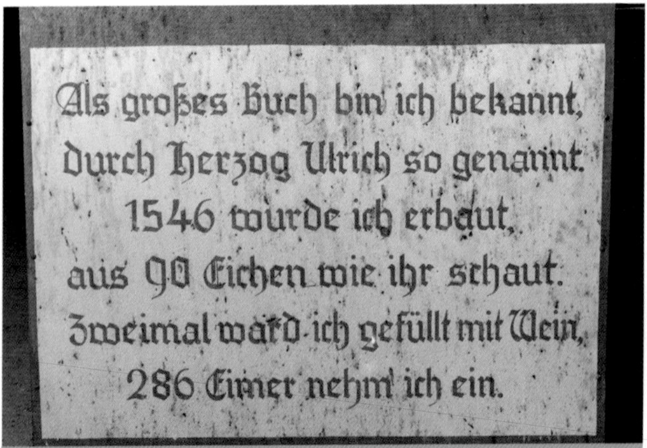

Als großes Buch bin ich bekannt,
Durch Herzog Ulrich so genannt.
1546 wurde ich erbaut,
aus 90 Eichen wie ihr schaut.
Zweimal ward ich gefüllt mit Wein,
286 Eimer nehm' ich ein.

Fig. 8   Poem on metal plate, around 1930

time so Tübingen became his preferred place of residence and seat of government alongside Stuttgart, the actual royal seat. He died in Tübingen after suffering from a long period of gout and found his final resting place in the Tübingen Collegiate Church (Fig. 10).[14]

Duke Ulrich was a typical tyrant with extramarital affairs, who did not so much as recoil from torturing or executing his own subjects. Anyone was a potential victim, no matter what social circles they belonged to: peasant, middle-class or even aristocratic. One act, however, resulted in irrevocable damage to himself and his name: the murder of his friend and stable master Hans von Hutten, probably by his own hand. Hutten had dared to make public his duke's

Von Gottes gnaden Ulrich Hertzog zu Wirtenberg vnd Deck Graff zů Mumpelgarten.

Fig. 9   Hans Brosamer: Duke Ulrich von Württemberg in armour, woodcut, about 1537

Fig. 10   Josef Schmid: Grave of Duke Ulrich von Württemberg, 1550;
Simon Schlör: Duchess Sabina von Württemberg, 1565

legitimate but immoral desire for his beautiful wife and
thereby exposed him to public ridicule. The result was
death for revenge and defamation. Against this background
of his faults and crimes, Ulrich's self-chosen motto, which
he already selected as a young man, resembles an oath of
disclosure, which underlines his militant, even brutal desire
for a self-determined future: "stat animo".[15] His motto can
be translated, on the one hand, in the sense of his thirst
for future actions: "I firmly intend to do it" and "I have it
in mind" and, on the other hand, in the understanding of
a moral steadfastness with "the purpose is clear" and "it
is decided". His deeds show in which way his maxim was
to be understood. History knows of his unprecedented

pompousness[16], his unpredictability in decisions, his thirst for adventure[17] and his unvarnished brutality, which, in combination with his violent temper and vindictiveness, had fatal consequences. All this led him into constant warfare and thus into great financial hardship, which resulted in the bankruptcy of the duchy.[18] In 1519, after a series of conflicts, the military conquest of the free imperial city Reutlingen ultimately put Ulrich into complete opposition to Emperor Maximilian I[st] (Fig. 11). As a consequence, the emperor imposed an imperial exile on him for breach of peace. His marriage was also marked by strife and violence. This led to an open break with his wife Sabina of Bavaria (1492–1564; Fig. 12), whom he never saw again after her flight to Bavaria. Throughout his life he put up a fight—even against his own subjects, as the Tübingen "Schandtafel", a kind of black list (Fig. 13), in the Museum at Hohentübingen Castle impressively proves.[19] Ulrich fought as an adolescent commander successfully in the Landshut War of Succession (1504–05), in the revolt of Poor Conrad (1514) against the rural population and was defeated by the Swabian League (1519), i.e. the urban-dominated upper class, the "Ehrbarkeit" of Württemberg, consisting of patricians, merchants and scholars. He was also later defeated in the Peasants' War (1525), later won Lauffen am Neckar (1534) and lost again in the Schmalkaldic War (1546). His greed for greatness, fame and power was very strong.[20] After his return from exile, Duke Ulrich, then a grown man, actively supported the cause of the Reformation from 1534 onwards. As proof for his Lutheranism, he chosed a new motto, which he adopted from the Saxon Electors and Martin Luther respectively: "Verbum Domini Manet in

Aeternum"—"The Word of the Lord will endure for ever". The short form, "V.D.M.I.E.", can still be found today on the upper left part of a banner coming from the mouth of a stag above the elaborately designed portal to the Great Hall at Hohentübingen Castle (Fig. 14). Ulrich verifiably interfered in the pressing ecclesiastical and social issues of his time. In this regard, he enacted an extensive land constitution (Fig. 15) in collaboration with his councillors and theologians in June 1536. It contained 40 main articles in which state and church norms were decreed. This constitution regulated not only moral discipline, but also provisions regarding public order, justice, and state sovereignty as well as trade, commerce and agriculture. The prohibitions included widespread drinking and drinking to excess, as well as card and dice games. It was principally these excesses and pleasures, especially gambling,[21] that the Duke himself indulged in, since such pleasures corresponded to the feudal understanding of representation at all courts of the Empire. An acute and widespread social problem at the time was excessive alcohol consumption. Such excesses raised the ecclesiastical-moral question of moderation and self-control—expressed in the Latin term "temperantia". Like other sovereign princes, Ulrich had single-sheet prints printed in the form of public orders against drunkenness.[22] However, these declarations only applied to the subjects. For himself, the Christian virtue of moderation was certainly not the first and foremost concern. In contrast, Ulrich's whole purpose was to increase his fame and the power of his house. What mattered most to him was:

"Gloria" (fame / honour) and "Victoria" (victory), "Auctoritas" (power / violence) and "Potestas" (rule / authority).

IMPERATOR
DIVVS MAXI
PIVS FELIX

CAESAR
MILIANVS
AVGVSTVS·

Fig. 11   Albrecht Dürer and Hans Weiditz the Younger: Emperor Maximilian I., woodcut, after 1519

Fig. 12 Barthel Beham: Sabina von Bayern, Wife of Duke Ulrich von Württemberg, panel, 1530, Munich

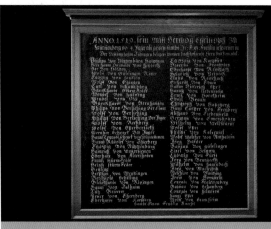

Fig. 13   "Schandtafel", black list, of Hohentübingen Castle, panel painting

Fig. 14   Detail of the portal to the Great Hall, courtyard of Hohentübingen
Castle

Des Fürstenthumbs
Wirtemberg newe Lands
ordnung.

Anno. M. D. XXXVI.

Fig. 15   Title page of the regional order, 1536, woodcut

Due to the competition between the princes in the empire, Ulrich, like other sovereigns, did everything possible[23] to publicly display his own claim to power via constructions, arts, rituals[24] and symbols, and, in doing so, to increase it. All the arts and media thus served the purpose of individual fame, which ideally led to an elevation of rank, i.e. to the elitist circle of the electors and princes. Duke Ulrich[25] used wars, tournaments and hunts for this purpose, as well as medals, coins, woodcuts and printed writings; traditionally also fortress and palace buildings as well as burials and epitaphs, plus ephemeral events such as weddings, court music performances and celebrations.[26] Whether the Tübingen Giant Barrel was built to store large quantities of wine especially for large celebrations and times of siege or whether it was intended from the very beginning to serve mainly as an object of aristocratic and courtly representation is no longer possible to determine with certainty from the sources. What is certain, however, is that, both in history and collective memory, the Tübingen Giant Barrel is closely knit with Ulrich's reign and his name, which underlines its function as a symbol within the court.

Today, the material and age of the barrel are well documented in a dendrochronological expert's report from 2018.[27] The study provides information on the time frame in which the oak trees were felled and mentions the large wooded area north of Tübingen, Schönbuch, as the possible region of origin. The oaks were felled between 1546 and 1550, but mostly in the winter of the years 1548–49 and 1549–50. The period between 1546 and 1550 referred to in the report corresponds to the year 1546 which was mentioned in the poem on the barrel quoted at the beginning.

But what do the sources say? Numerous handwritten documents on the Tübingen Giant Barrel have been preserved in the Hauptstaatsarchiv Stuttgart in various bundles and contexts. An account book from 1549 to 1550 (Fig. 16) documents the payment for the Tübingen Giant Barrel at the price of 399 Folio.[28] Almost at the beginning, more precisely in third place under the category "craftsmen", there is a seven-line entry which mentions the payment to the cooper Master Simon Binder for the Tübingen Giant Barrel, thus confirming the dating from the dendrochronological report: 1549–50.

The question of whether the date from the previously quoted poem, "1546", indicates initial plans, contracts or even the actual start of construction of the barrel, requires the consultation of further sources. In a bundle of writings, which are summarised under the title "Tübingen secular" in the Hauptstaatsarchiv Stuttgart, there is an internal bundle consisting of four documents: two letters, one contract and an undated "consultation".[29] In a letter, dated 14 May 1546, Hans von Ow[30], in his position as castellan of Hohentübingen Castle, turns to his friend Jakob Brenig [Breuning?], secretary in the law office in Stuttgart. The starting point of his letter is an intended agreement („verschreybung") which Wilhelm Kohn[31] is to draw up at the "Rentkammer" (the office which was responsible for the administration of the income of the sovereign in early modern Württemberg) for the "making and production of a large barrel" by Master Simon Binder. The letter states that within the agreement, the cooper is to "predicate himself and guarantee" that the Tübingen Giant Barrel is paid for only after its production and installation and after it has been filled with wine with-

Rechnung

Unser Wilhaelm Khünen vnd boeff vonackhers baider verwallter der Landschreiberey zu Stuet garten. Das wir von berürter Landschreiberey wegen eingenomen vnd ausgeben haben von Georij Anno dm xlix Inclusiue Bis wider Georij Anno dm xl L exclusiue

out leaking. Through the castellan of Tübingen, the cooper asks for an advance of 100 guilders for his first work and the wood from the Stuttgart treasury of the "Rentkammer".

In the second letter, dated 4 October 1546, Duke Ulrich is told of the arrival of Master Simon Binder and his servants in Tübingen. Under continuous work—"day and night"—the "large barrel" was assembled in the cellars of the castle. During this time, the cooper together with his two or three servants spent nights at the Blaubeurer Hof—today known as the Nonnenhaus. However, the question of "food" was open as to whether the craftsmen from "Benickhain" (Bönnigheim) should be provided with food at the Duke's expense.[32]

Handtwercksleuten

Item iij gld xxrj rdr Wolff Zinckeisen, ...
... zu Stütgarten für allerlay arbeit der Canntzley stall gemacht. Vom xij
December anno ... plaiy biß den xvj
tag ... ... thut iij gld xxrj

Item iij gld xbrj rdr Hainrich Scheren,
... zu Stütgarten für allerlay arbeit
... meister abrechnung ... Canntzley
stall ... Rosstall gemacht ... ...
... nach Cantate anno ... ...
... ... thut iij gld xbrj rdr

Item iij ... gld ... Schreiner Hanns, ...
... ... zu ... ...
... dem grossen kasten ... ...
... ...
... thut iij ... rdr

Item x gld plaiy ... Anna Hamerin,
... ... von der Kamer,
... ... anno ... ...
... thut x gld ... rdr

Item ... gld xxrj rdr Cunraten Forsth,
... Schreiner ... Stütgarten von dem
Balmhofen, ... der ... ...
anno ... ...
... thut ... gld xrj rdr

Summa ... gld xxx rdr

THE MASTER OF THE GIANT BARREL

It is conspicuous that the poem quoted at the beginning mentions the ducal constituent but not the builder of the Giant Barrel. Apparently, the latter was no longer generally known at the end of the nineteenth century and was almost forgotten. All the more tempting to look for the master craftsman of the Tübingen Giant Barrel, which is why two further previously unpublished handwritten sources are presented here that provide information about the life and work of the master.

In the Stuttgart Book of Accounts (Fig. 17) from the years 1549–50, two "Landschreiber", accountants in early modern Württemberg, who were responsible for recording and accounting for the sovereign's income, Wilhelm Kühn and Wolf Bonacker, mention the master of the barrel:

Craftsmen
[...]
Also 384 guilders were paid to Master Simon
Binder, citizen of Beninghaus [sic]
for the large barrel in Tübingen
which holds 47 cart loads of wine.
Made by order of our gracious Sovereign and Lord
Reached an agreement due to his receipt
With the 'Rentkammer'.[33]

This central source for the Tübingen Giant Barrel contains important information about the builder, the cost and the size of the barrel. The cooper Simon Binder is mentioned here as the master craftsman. While coopers are generally called "Küfer" in German, these craftsmen are also known as "Böttcher" in Southern Germany (Fig. 18). Simon Binder probably came from the town of Bönnigheim in today's district of Ludwigsburg. Although the source at this point is in need of interpretation due to the corrupted spelling of the place name "Beninghaus", it is very likely that today's Bönnigheim is the cooper's place of origin. This interpretation is supported by another historical source which has only been preserved in a copy by Financial Councillor Rudolf Moser from 1833 in the Staatsarchiv Ludwigsburg. In a so-called "Accord" (contract), which was drawn up on 15 May 1546, Duke Ulrich had the commission to Master Simon Binder to build a giant barrel recorded in writing.[34] According to this written commission, the cooper from Bönnigheim produced thus two larges barrels in the same year, both for Hohenasperg Fortress and Hohentübingen Castle. The proximity between Bönnigheim and Hohenasperg Fortress—a distance of about 20 kilometres (Fig. 19)—suggests that the contract was awarded to a regional master and thus to Simon Binder, the cooper from Bönnigheim. Consequently, the corrupted place name in the Stuttgart Book of Accounts of 1549–50 should be read as Bönnigheim.

Der Bütner.

Ich bin ein Bütner / vnd mach stolz/
Auß Förhen / Tennen / Eichen Holz/
Badwañ / Schmalzkübl / scheffel vñ geltn/
Die Bütten vnd Weinfässer / weltn/
Bier Fässer machn / bichen vnd binden/
Waschzübr thut man bey mir finden/
Auch mach ich Lägl / Fässer vnd Stäbch/
Gen Franckfurt / Leipzig vnd Lübig.

90

Fig. 18   Jost Amman: Der Bütner, woodcut, in: Hans Sachs, Eygentliche
Beschreibung aller Stände, Frankfurt 1568

Fig. 19   Johann Scheubel: Warhafftige und grundtliche Abconterpheung des
loblichen Fürstenthumbs Würtemberg, Tübingen 1559, woodcut

Anno 1547. ward der Universitet hauß zu Tüwing ...

... Anno 1547. nova hec ædes, ...

A.o 1533. ... Anno 1535. hat H. Hertzog Ulrich von Wirtenberg, d. alt schloß zu Tüwing abbrechen ...

... M. Diman ein Biesser von Binnigheim an N ... A. 1548.

Fig. 20   Volgt ein Verzaichnus, allerhand fürnemmer, in und an der stadt Tüwing, fürgenommenen gebaue, 17th century

THE VOLUME AND THE WOOD OF THE BARREL

The capacity of the large barrel in the Hohenasperg Fortress is stated in the "Accord" of 1546 with 40 cart loads or 240 buckets. Today, this corresponds to about 70,390 litres. This means that its volume is exactly 7 cart loads or 36 buckets smaller than the Giant Barrel in Tübingen, which holds about 80.950 litres.[35] Simon Binder received as payment full board during the time the barrel was constructed and, for his craftmanship and building material, 330 guilders from his duke. In contrast, the Stuttgart Book of Accounts puts the cost of the Tübingen Giant Barrel at 384 guilders. The comparison with the sunken giant barrel of Hohenasperg Fortress shows that the Tübingen Giant Barrel was 54 guilders more expensive. This can certainly be explained by its larger volume, more material and a higher labour input. Adding a third manuscript from the seventeenth century, which contains a list of buildings in the city of Tübingen,[36] one can read next to the marginal note "large barrel" (Fig. 20) that Simon, the cooper from Bönnigheim am Neckar, built a large barrel in the years from 1546 to 1548. As payment, he received a court dress and 150 guilders. The latter was crossed out by another hand and changed to the entry "330" guilders, which incorrectly states the amount for the barrel at Hohenasperg. Likewise, the year 1548 was specified by the subsequent addition: "[15]46", which

Fig. 21   Jörg Syrlin the Elder: Choir Stalls, Ulm Minster, 1469–1474

results in a rather long period of about three years—starting from the beginning of construction to final works and improvements—for the barrel of Tübingen. Furthermore, there is a longer addition, a margin at the edge of the page. According to this, the cooper made the barrel at his own expense and then set it up in Tübingen. On top of that, he supposedly had given a guarantee of 80, 90 or 100 years on his product. This long guarantee is doubted by "Master Mayer", who obtained the position of court cooper.[37] Instead, he assumes a ten-year guarantee. However, in order for the barrel to remain sealed, the felled wood should have been dried six to seven years prior to its use, which was not done. There is also information about the material:

Fig. 22   Wenzel Dietrich: Coffered Ceiling, 1585, Fugger Castle, Kirchheim an der Mindel

90 logs were needed to build the barrel, which are said to have been felled in "Rutenhammer", i.e. in Rutesheim near Leonberg. These subsequent additions to the edge of the paper are, with their critically commenting tone and their factually supplementary content, an indication that the Tübingen Giant Barrel remained a topic of discussion among court servants—especially coopers—even after about a hundred years, as the tightness of the Giant Barrel was a permanent problem. A second filling of the barrel seems to have taken place in the seventeenth century, as indicated by the passage at the end of the manuscript: "it was filled with wine in this year, it keeps tight". High sums of money paid for large and artistic works made of wood

were not only a sign of the financial power and high social standing of the clients, but also indicated the uniqueness and fame of the crafted object. Since no other giant barrel from the first half of the sixteenth century besides the one from Tübingen has survived, and since only younger barrels are known based on sources both inside[38] and outside Württemberg, only other well-known examples can be used here. Thus, the famous Ulm Choir Stalls (Fig. 21) by the carver Jörg Syrlin the Elder (1425–91), which were made between 1469 and 1474, i.e. in a period of six years, cost the impressive sum of 1188 guilders.[39] No less well known is the much praised coffered ceiling (Fig. 22) by the master carpenter Wenzel Dietrich of Augsburg (c. 1535 to c. 1622) in the Fugger Castle at Kirchheim an der Mindel in Swabia, for which the immense sum of 3300 guilders was paid in 1585.[40] Duke Ulrich spent, of course, the largest sums on his wars and fortresses. For only the expansion and conversion of Hohentübingen until 1540, the citizens paid 64.387 guilders to the Duke.[41] In contrast to these immense sums, the 384 guilders paid for the Tübingen Giant Barrel are almost modest. If one compares the cost of the Giant Barrel with that of harnesses (Fig. 23) commissioned by Duke Ulrich, some of which from the well-known workshop of the armourer Wilhelm von Worms (d. 1538) in Nuremberg according to an invoice from 1510 in which 108 guilders were paid, it is clear that 100 guilders were a large sum in the early modern period.[42] In another example, Martin Luther received an annual income of 100 guilders from the Saxon elector Friedrich III the Wise before his marriage. The artist Albrecht Dürer is also said to have received a "Leibgeding", a pension in the early modern period, of 100 guilders a year from Emperor Maximilian[st]. In Nuremberg, a landsknecht was usually paid four guilders a month, i.e. 48 guilders a year, and a maid five guilders a year. These examples show that Duke Ulrich, in spite of immense debts, always made costly expenditures, nonetheless.

Fig. 23   Wilhelm von Worms: harness, 1510, Nürnberg

Fig. 24 Narcissus Schwelin: Kleine Würtembergische Chronica […], Stuttgart 1660

"LARGE BARREL" AND "LARGE BOOK"

By the seventeenth and eighteenth century, important facts about the Tübingen Giant Barrel had already been forgotten and replaced by others. For example, the much-cited chronicle (Fig. 24) of the Württemberg official and councillor Narcissus Schwelin (1588–1669) from 1660 contains the early news that the cooper received the sum of 150 guilders and a court dress from the duke for the construction of the barrel in 1548.[43] The reference to the court dress as well as the 150 guilders seem to have been taken from the previously presented manuscript of the seventeenth century.[44] Both statements turned out to be persistent. From then on, they can be found in almost all historical works and town chronicles about Tübingen.[45]

Similarly, Andreas Christoph Zeller (1684–1743), the Württemberg councillor and prelate of Anhausen Abbey, reproduced these details which have now become facts in his "Merkwürdigkeiten" (Fig. 25) from the year 1743.[46] He added the name of the master craftsman but mentioned a wrong location: "The name of the cooper was Simon and he was from Bietigheim."[47] New, however, is the comparison of the Giant Barrel with a book: "that it [the Giant Barrel] could not be a real book, especially not the Confessio Würtembergica".[48] The literary starting point for the comparison between barrel and book was, as Zeller himself

Ausführliche

Merckwürdigkeiten

der

Hochfürstl. Würtembergischen

UNIVERSITÆT

und

Stadt

Tübingen,

betreffend

Dessen Alterthum/ Pfaltzgräfl. und Würtembergische Herrschafften,

innerlich=und äusserliche Verfassung, Jurisdiction, Privilegien, Hofgericht, Kirchen, Collegia und Stipendia mit ihren Ordnungen , Succession deren Professorum, auch allerhand Begebenheiten zu Kriegs= und Friedens=Zeiten , nebst vermischten Anmerckungen, rc.
kürtzlich doch umständlich beschrieben

von

Andreas Christoph Zellern/

Hochfürstlich. Würtemb. Rath und Prälaten des Closters Anhausen.

TUBINGEN

In der Bergerischen Buchhandlung.

Fig. 25   Andreas Christoph Zeller: Ausführliche Merckwürdigkeiten der [...] und Stadt Tübingen [...], Tübingen 1743

states, a disputation in Tübingen in 1677. It was headed
by the candidate Johann Ludwig Metz (1648–89 or 1691)[49]
and his examiner Balthasar Raith (1616–83), who was a
professor of theology in Tübingen. This exam was published
as a dissertation (Fig. 26),[50] so that the section "Problema
[...] Of the large book in Tübingen", which is important for
the Tübingen Giant Barrel, is summarised here: On the
problem ("frequentatum hoc ore omnium"), which was
already much talked about at that time, which referred to
the very large book ("grandis ille liber") of Tübingen and
in which library it was kept, in the castle's library, or in the
Collegium Illustre or the university library, Metz replies that
this could be the thick volume containing the Duke's con-
fession together with the apologetic writings of Johannes
Benz, Jakob Beuerlin, Jakob Heerbrand, Johannes Isenmann
and Dietrich Schnepf against Pedro de Soto. He closes his
remarks with the almost show-like sentence that he is much
more certain ("multo certius id est") that the so-called large
barrel "Grande DOLIUM" of Tübingen is kept in the cellar of
the princely castle ("in Cella Ducal").[51] At the very end, he
cites the chronicle of Nariccius Schwelin as the source for
his explanations, thus completing the circle.

In the following recapitulation by the theologian and
historian Ludwig Melchior Fischlin (1672–1729) "Memoria
Theologorum Wirtembergensium" (Fig. 27) from 1710[52],
Johann Ludwig Metz's playful comparison of the large
barrel with Duke Ulrich's large book is still adopted, with
reference to its hypothetical character, but hereafter this
assumption becomes a fact. From now on, in almost all
works of historiography—as a synonym, as equation and
witty anecdote—the Giant Barrel is also referred to as the

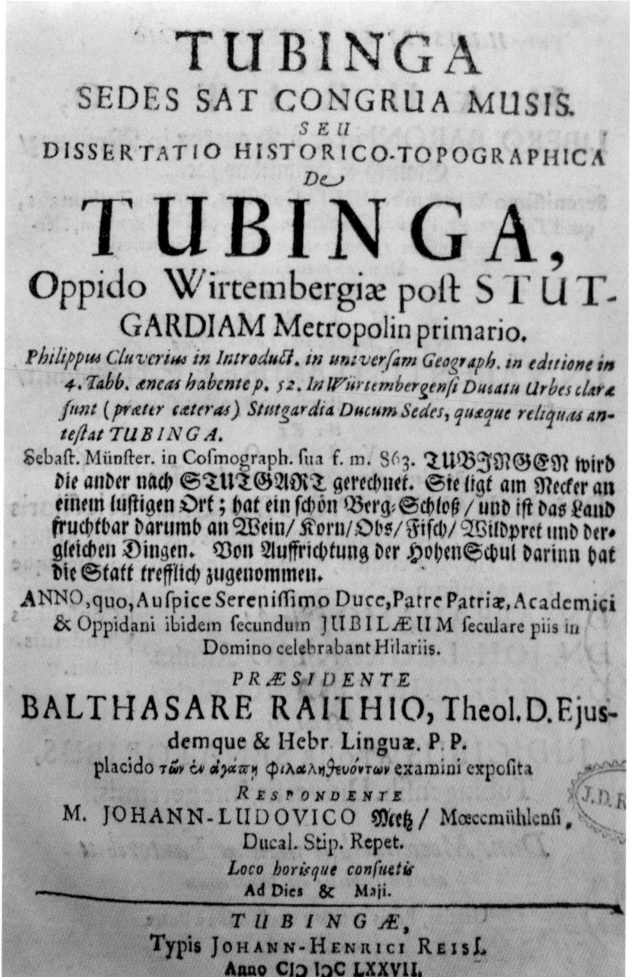

TUBINGA

SEDES SAT CONGRUA MUSIS.

SEU

DISSERTATIO HISTORICO-TOPOGRAPHICA

De

TUBINGA,

Oppido Wirtembergiæ post STUT-GARDIAM Metropolin primario.

Philippus Cluverius in Introduct. in universam Geograph. in editione in 4. Tabb. æneas habente p. 52. In Würtembergensi Ducatu Urbes claræ sunt (præter cæteras) Stutgardia Ducum Sedes, quæque reliquas antestat TUBINGA.

Sebast. Münster. in Cosmograph. sua f. m. 863. ₮ᵘᵇᶦⁿᵍᵉⁿ wird die ander nach Stutgart gerechnet. Sie ligt am Necker an einem lustigen Ort; hat ein schön Berg-Schloß / und ist das Land fruchtbar darumb an Wein/ Korn/ Obs/ Fisch/ Wildpret und dergleichen Dingen. Von Auffrichtung der HohenSchul darinn hat die Statt trefflich zugenommen.

ANNO, quo, Auspice Sereniſſimo Duce, Patre Patriæ, Academici & Oppidani ibidem secundum JUBILÆUM seculare piis in Domino celebrabant Hilariis.

PRÆSIDENTE

BALTHASARE RAITHIO, Theol. D. Ejusdemque & Hebr. Linguæ. P. P.

placido τῶν ἐν ἀγάπῃ φιλαληθευόντων examini exposita

RESPONDENTE

M. JOHANN-LUDOVICO Metz / Mœccmühlensi, Ducal. Stip. Repet.

Loco horisque consuetis
Ad Dies & Maji.

TUBINGÆ,
Typis JOHANN-HENRICI REISII.
Anno CIↃ IↃC LXXVII.

Fig. 26 Johann Ludwig Metz: Tubinga sedes sat congrua musis seu dissertatio historico-topographica de Tubinga [...], Tübingen [Univ. Diss.] 1677

"large book" of Tübingen. Thus, a theological joke turned into truth in the end.[53]

The fact that the Tübingen Giant Barrel remained alive as a local historical monument in the minds of some authors and historians as well as noblemen and court servants during the eighteenth century was probably above all due to the then current events in other places, such as the construction of a large barrel in Ludwigsburg Palace. It was finished between 1719 and 1721 and has a volume of 90,000 litres.[54] But also in other principalities, new giant barrels were built. A prestigious duel broke out between the rulers. Everyone wanted to have the largest barrel and so the competition began. At that time, the theology student Johann Benjamin Wolff[55] published his paper „Teutschlandes Dreyfaches Denckmahl des Fruchtbahren Weinstockes: Das ist, Gründliche Beschreibung, Der drey Grossen Wein-Fässer in Europa" (Fig. 28) in 1717, in which he describes three principalities as well as the largest and best-known barrels of Heidelberg, Halberstadt and Königstein to pay homage to their potentates. This was an obvious attempt to recommend himself for higher tasks and offices, for which the subject of the large barrels was suitable, since they were held in high esteem and were talked about at court. Wolff particularly praised the noble Saxony, which is why the laurel went to the large barrel, built in 1680, in Königstein.[56] It was, however, the large barrel (Fig. 29) in the Heidelberg Castle of the Electors of the Electoral Palatinate which caused a sensation in the empire, as it was praised and celebrated in writing and pictures for many generations. It was built for the first time in 1591, held 132 cart loads (about 127,000 litres) and disintegrated during the Thirty Years' War.

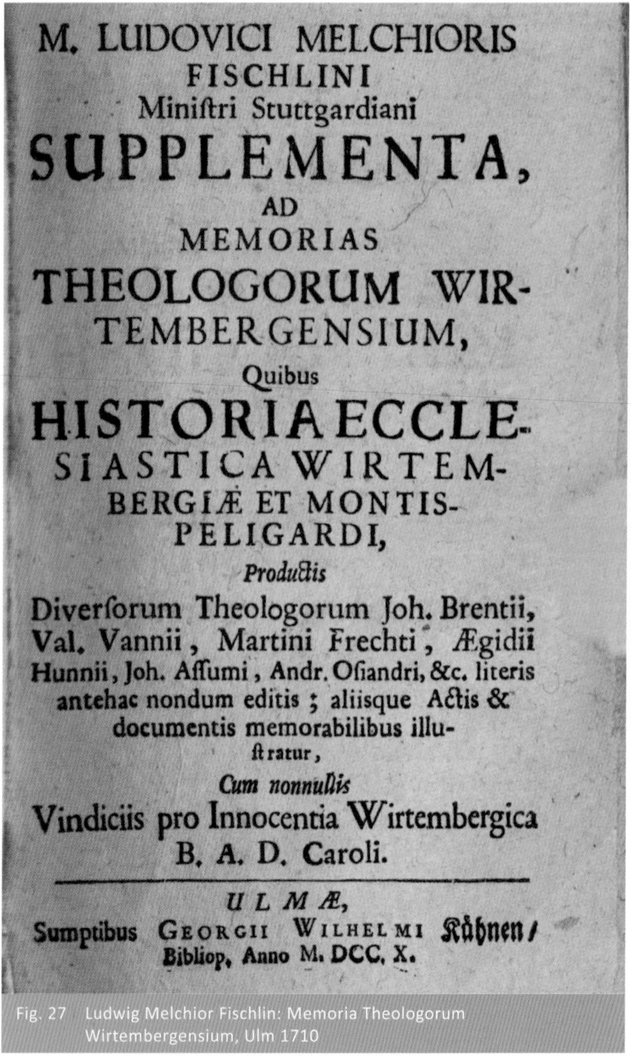

M. LUDOVICI MELCHIORIS FISCHLINI

Miniſtri Stuttgardiani

SUPPLEMENTA,

AD
MEMORIAS

THEOLOGORUM WIR-TEMBERGENSIUM,

Quibus

HISTORIA ECCLE-SIASTICA WIRTEM-BERGIÆ ET MONTIS-PELIGARDI,

Produ&is

Diverſorum Theologorum Joh. Brentii,
Val. Vannii, Martini Frechti, Ægidii
Hunnii, Joh. Aſſumi, Andr. Oſiandri, &c. literis
antehac nondum editis ; aliisque Actis &
documentis memorabilibus illu-
ſtratur,

Cum nonnullis

Vindiciis pro Innocentia Wirtembergica
B. A. D. Caroli.

ULMÆ,
Sumptibus GEORGII WILHELMI Kühnen/
Bibliop, Anno M. DCC. X.

Fig. 27 Ludwig Melchior Fischlin: Memoria Theologorum
Wirtembergensium, Ulm 1710

Teutschlandes
Dreyfaches
Denckmahl
des Fruchtbahren Weinstockes.
Das ist/
Gründliche

Beschreibung/
Der drey Grossen
Wein-Fässer in EUROPA,
nebst ausführlicher
RELATION
von der
Berg-Vestung Königstein/
wie auch
Der vornehmsten Städte und Schlösser / des
Chur-Fürstenthumbs Sachßen / der Chur-Pfaltz/
und des Fürstenthumbs Halberstadt.

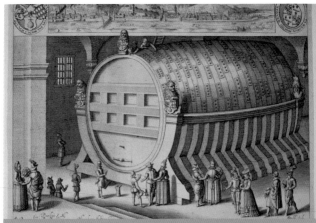

Fig. 29   Jacob de Gheyn, Willem Jacobsz Delff, Hendrik van Haestens: VAS
STUPENDAE MAGNITVDINIS, engraving, Heidelberg 1608

A second large barrel was made in Heidelberg in 1664,
containing 204 cartloads (about 195,000 litres), but it also
fell apart. Thus, in the eighteenth century, first a third barrel
was produced in the years 1724 to 1728 with about 202,000
litres and finally even a fourth large barrel in 1751 with 236
cart loads, about 221,726 litres. As answer to the barrel in
Heidelberg, the Saxon elector Friedrich August I the Strong
(1670–1733), as August II King of Poland, effectively in competition with the electoral princes of the Palatinate, had an
even larger barrel (Fig. 30) built at his fortress Königstein
in Saxony with a volume of about 238,600 litres in 1725[57].
This is what bloodless victories look like.Compared to the

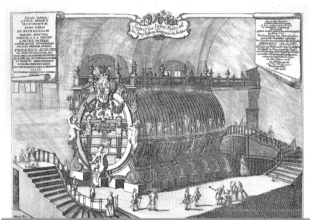

Fig. 30 C. G. Nitsche: Prospect des Großen Faßes auf der BergVestung Königstein in Sachsen, Kupferstich, around 1750

volume of the Tübingen Giant Barrel, the capacity of the wine barrel of Königstein had tripled.

In accordance with the knowledge that the princes were in competition for the largest and most magnificent prestige objects, the princely giant barrels can be associated with the well-known term "parade". During the eighteenth century, this term was used as a prefix for princely parade rooms, parade carriages and parade beds, which particularly and especially had to serve the courtly splendour and representation. The princely giant barrels belong to precisely this courtly context, so that it is justified to speak of them as parade barrels.[58] It was with these that the proverbial great state—grand état—was to be made, i.e. to achieve prestige and splendour.

Even though the first written evidence of the specific and playful equation of the "large barrel" with the "large book" can be found in the Tübingen Disputation of 1677, it can be assumed that it initially originated in Fischart's *Geschichtklitterung*. The popularity of the synonymous use of the word in Tübingen as early as the sixteenth century is indicated not only by Johann Ludwig Metz's statement: "frequentatum hoc ore omnium" (this repetition is on everyone's lips), but also by a passage in Johann Fischart's *Geschichtklitterung* from 1582, in which he briefly refers to the "large book of Tübingen", without, however, clarifying which concrete theological work could be meant by the latter and without direct reference to the Tübingen Barrel.[59] But which circumstance, which concrete phenomenon on the barrel could have served as starting point and impulse for this popular way of speaking?

A glance inside the barrel shows (Fig. 31) that it is filled with countless names and dates. Most letters and numbers are written in white chalk. Almost no spot is free and the writings often overlap each other. The result is a picture that is unparalleled. Today, it is only speculative whether visitors who squeezed through the narrow bunghole were actually allowed to immortalise themselves in the barrel or whether these actions were merely tolerated. However, it is a fact that for more than 350 years, guests did not sign the guest book during barrel tours and feasts in the barrel, but the barrel. The two oldest legible dates in the barrel are "1579" and "1589" and one of the most recent "1956" (Fig. 32). In this way, the Tübingen Giant Barrel received a new

Fig. 31   Inside of the Giant Barrel with the author

function. It became the longest openly displayed guest book in the country, perhaps even in the realm.—Even today, it is told that Johann Wolfgang von Goethe visited the Giant Barrel during his visit of the Castle in Tübingen on 9 September 1797. However, as long as his name is not found in the barrel, this will, for lack of evidence, probably remain a legend. While the presumption that this special cultural-historical practice of entering names in the "large barrel" or the "large book" is the actual starting point for the popular equation of barrel and book seems to be obvious, it can only be assumed in the end.

Fig. 32a Tübingen Giant Barrel with dates on the Inside

Fig. 32b Tübingen Giant Barrel with dates on the Inside

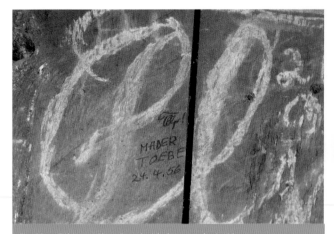

Fig. 32c   Tübingen Giant Barrel with dates on the Inside

A PLACE OF INTEREST:
PICTURES OF THE GIANT BARREL

The publication by Georg Braun and Franz Hogenberg "Civitates orbis terrarum", richly illustrated with masterly copper engravings, contains the first printed graphic representation of the city of Tübingen along with the castle and the Giant Barrel (Fig. 33). Its four volumes were printed between 1572 and 1588 and were subsequently published several times in new editions.[60] The accompanying text in the fourth volume from 1588, which describes the city of Tübingen and its history, contains no reference to the Giant Barrel. Only in general terms and in a theme characteristic of Tübingen, the topography, such as the vineyard hills "vinifero colle" and the castle "arce", is briefly mentioned at the very beginning.[61]

However, the text is mainly about the university and its professors. The veduta is harmoniously arranged. The view of the city is divided into four zones. In the foreground are mostly people working at the wine harvest and several stacks of wood, which symbolize the rafting craft and timber trade at the Neckar. The centre is marked by the river with active fishermen and the stone bridge. The town with its fortified walls, numerous houses and the collegiate church towering above everything is in the background. Slightly set off from the town, higher and situated without obstruction, the seat of the Duke, the proud Hohentübingen

Fig. 33   Tubinga / Tubingen, copperplate engraving, in: Georg Braun and
Franz Hogenberg, Civitates orbis terrarum, Cologne 1588, Bd. 4

GEN

BINGE

Castle is enthroned. The fourth zone is formed by the sky with its moving cloud images, which contribute significantly to the vividness of the landscape. The composition of the picture relinquishes a strict symmetry. The different emphasis between left and right is striking. Both the town crest and the cartouche with the name of the city are slightly shifted to the right into the sphere of the city, so that the left side with the castle takes up much more space in the picture. The princely sphere and the bourgeois site are thus weighted differently in the picture's message.

The dichotomy of the picture observed here also applies for the foreground. While the working population is shown on the left, doing their daily work under the Duke's seat, i.e. under his regency, a large barrel with two richly dressed persons, who obviously do not do any work, is seen on the right. The striking placement of a barrel at the very front, on the right of the picture implicates its importance. The imposing size and the ownership of the barrel is clearly indicated. The two richly clad persons of rank, the lady, seen head-on with a purse on her belt and the gentleman, seen from behind with a precious dagger, are facing each other in conversation. On the one hand, they serve as a standard of comparison for the large barrel, which is almost twice their size, and on the other, they represent the feudal world to which the large barrel belongs as well. This distribution of the picture clearly indicates a chiastic pictorial rhetoric, in which the spheres of the nobility and the citizens, which were marked by the spheres of the castle on the left and the city on the right, are now exchanged in the foreground. In this masterful engraving, the Tübingen Giant Barrel was probably depicted for the first time in picture form in 1572.

The Giant Barrel is only acknowledged in picture and not in written form in the accompanying text, which could indicate that in the sixteenth century there was—apart from its brief mention in Johann Fischart's *Geschichtklitterung* in 1575— probably only a popular and thus oral account that contributed to its fame. Only towards the end of the sixteenth century, a wood cut turned up (Fig. 34) which contains both the city veduta of Tübingen as well as a textual mention of the Giant Barrel. The Tübingen Print, dated 1590, was made by the artist Jonathan Sauter and printed by Alexander Hock in the Burgsteige in Tübingen.[62] The topographical view was certainly based on the at that time well known and much appreciated copper engraving from "Civitates orbis terrarum", albeit with some variations and reductions. This is most evident in details such as the sequence, order and grouping of trees and bushes along the Neckar in the area below the castle. Of interest here, however, is not so much the simple woodcut as the poem:

"[...]
A princely castle is also built,
With towers, moat, fortification and walls.
On top of a mountain of this city,
which is now named after it,
Two lions old, a really large barrel,
Which holds 47 cart loads.
[...]"

With this brief mention of the Giant Barrel including its capacity in the form of a poem of praise to the "famous princely town of Tübingen", the combined and thus mutu-

Tübingen/die ander Fürstlich Statt/
  Ein weitberümpten namen sie hat.
Sie lige in einem lustigen Teych/
  Dazu strecken sich vil Thäler gleich.
Necker/Ammer/Lustnawer Thal/
  Steinacher vnnd vil ander ohn zal.
Zwen Flüß schnell durch die Thäler rinnen/
  Vnd der Statt grossen nutzen bringen.
Der Necker/Ammer/seind sie genande/
  Dem Fischer Handewerck wolbekande.
Fruchtbar seind Thäler mit Wiesen grund/
  Mit Obs gewechsen auß menschen fund.
Die Berg seind fruchtbar in disem ort/
  Wölche mier selten ondultma erhört.

Ein Fürstlich Schloß ist auch gebawen/
  Mit Thürnen/Graben/vest vnd Mauren.
Oben auff ein Berg diser Statt/
  Wölcher von ihm jetzt den Namen hat.
Zwen Löwen ale/ein gar grosses Faß/
  Wölchs 47. Füder helt an der Maß.
Auch vil hubsch oreig wer den gesunden/
  Ab welchem einer sich möcht verwunden.

Es ist ziemlich gr...
Mit Korn v...
Wein/Fisch/Ob...
Rechter Pfer...
So vil sich diser...
Wer sie niche f...
Wiewol sie verg...
Mit Bawen
Wann niche die...
In diser Sta...
Von Graff Eb...
Dem Hochge...
Als man Tausen...
Siben vnnd ...
Von tag zu tag...
Als gelebtr...
Vier Doccores...
Wölch all an...
Siben erfahren...
Auch drey...
Freye Künst se...
Wölch Tuge...

Aula noua   Pfar kirch   Oſerberg

wayd/	Vrſach der ding vnd warheit bringen.
y getreyd.	Reden von ſachen mit guten ſinnen.
kommen/	Wie ſie all in Summa werden genendt/
rdt genomen.	Mit rechtem Studieren mansbaß erkendt.
w belange/	Vil Gelehrter Leut werden erzogen/
bek andt.	Die ihrer Kunſt halb ſeindhoch zuloben.
aſſen/	Im vier vnd Sechzigen ſein cedirt/
eren laſſen.)	Vierzehen Doctor in tituliert.
geſtiſſt/	Vier in Heiliger Göttlicher gſchriſſt/
auff gericht.	Vier in Rechten gar wol vnderricht.
em Bart/	Sechs in der Artzney wol erfahren/
ter ward.	Wölchen Gott wöll alln jr gſundheit ſparen.
dere zale/	Vnnd den gmeinen nutz vorbehalten/
halde.	Daß ſie den fleiſſig thun ver walten/
mnen/	Daß ſie zur Seel auch fridlich leben/
kommen.	Wie es die ſchwachheit Sleybs möcht geben.
ſchriffe/	Wölchen alln Gott ſein gnad verleyh/
vettriſſt/	Das wir all kommen ins Himmelreich.
rechten/	Welches vns von anfang iſt bereit/
ſchlechſten/	Von nun an biß in ewigkeit.
ren/	
en lehren.	Getruckt zu Tübingen/bey Alexander Hock/im jar 1590·

ally enhancing appreciation of the Giant Barrel in words and pictures begins. At the beginning of the twentieth century, the picture of the Giant Barrel experienced a new boom. This interest in the "good old days" began in the nineteenth century, triggered and sustained by literature and images of the Neckar Romanticism[63] (Fig. 35). An important name and initiator of the Neckar Romanticism was the well-known Stuttgart poet Gustav Schwab (1792–1850), who essentially conjured this dynamic by writing about it. Local authors also liked to take up medieval themes, such as the editor of the Tübingen Chronicle Eduard Morasch (1870–1918), who wrote a play revolving around the large barrel, which was based on the idea of a costumed carnival play and a "Bürgerfest", a public festival for all classes.[64]

Medieval castles and cities became more and more fashionable towards the end of the nineteenth century as tourism grew, even among a wider public. Especially medieval or supposedly medieval monuments and motives on postcards were increasingly applauded and widely distributed. This is how German buildings, monuments and works of art became known to the general public. In this way—nolens volens—every postcard writer contributed to the creation of a collective image of the past. By buying and sending a postcard with a historical motif, people not only showed their wanderlust and cosmopolitanism but also their attachment to their homeland and their interest in history to those who stayed at home. Thus, the personal greeting from afar became a vote for the most popular, most interesting and most fascinating historical monument.

Initiators and producers of the new mass medium of the postcard came from Tübingen. It was the postcard pub-

Fig. 35   Ludwig Meyer (drawn) und J. Axmann (engraved): Tübingen, steel engraving, in: G. Schwab, Wanderungen durch
Schwaben, Leipzig 1837

lishing house of the brothers Heinrich and Gustav Metz,
which produced their own postcard motives since 1896
and belonged to one of the largest of that branch within
Germany.[65] The Tübingen publishing house also used local
motifs:[66] the old town on the banks of the Neckar, the
town hall on the market square, the Collegiate Church and
Hohentübingen Castle with its prominent monument of the
lower castle gate.

The motif of the Giant Barrel also found its way into this
circle of scenes of Tübingen (Figs. 36–42). Between 1900
and 1950, the Metz publishing house in Tübingen produced several postcards with the motif of the Giant Barrel in
the castle cellar. This not only speaks for the fact that the

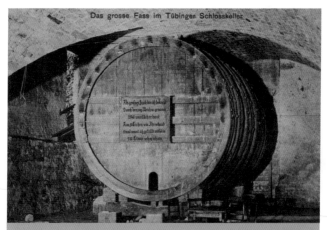

Das grosse Fass im Tübinger Schlosskeller

Fig. 36   Postcard, Publisher Gebrüder Metz, Tübingen around 1950

barrel could be visited, but also for its popularity in tourist circles at the time. Two postcard motives of the barrel can be distinguished. One shows only the Giant Barrel (Figs. 36–37), thus honouring it as a historical monument. Others show the barrel together with people. This was done to both emphasize the size and illustrate the fun of the—here mostly male—visitors during the tour.

Such genre-like scenes were very popular. They can be found in many variations published by the Metz brothers. Staffage figures were inserted by means of assembly and retouching.[67] This technique was used for the barrel motif, as can easily be seen in a comparison of the pictures (Figs. 38–39). A pair was inserted into the picture on the far left:

Fig. 37 Postcard, Publisher Gebrüder Metz, Tübingen around 1950

the lady with a large flower hat and the gentleman with a melon as headdress.

For such purposes, the publishing house created a repertoire of figure photos, which were intended to give the postcards not only liveliness, but also a specific atmosphere and mood. The fact that many picture postcards from the barrel with different constellations of people have been preserved to this day bears witness to the success of this concept of picture montage. A funny scene was repeatedly depicted and can be found in various postcards (Figs. 38–42).

It is clearly visible on the cards that a boy (Fig. 40), and several times a fraternity student with his characteristic

Fig. 38   Postcard, Publisher Gebrüder Metz, Tübingen around 1917

Fig. 39   Postcard, Publisher Gebrüder Metz, Tübingen around 1904

Fig. 40   Postcard, Publisher Gebrüder Metz, Tübingen, send 21 Juni 1908

Tübingen, Schloss.

9327   Das grosse Fass im Schlosskeller.

Fig. 41   Postcard, Publisher Gebrüder Metz, send 16 Oktober 1901

cap, look out of the bunghole. It is quite possible that students from corporate associations and fraternities were approached as potential buyers in the interest of customer identification. It is noticeable that several chalk drawings in the barrel originate from corps students who liked to immortalise themselves with the so-called Zirkel (Fig. 32), a monogram-like identification mark of the respective fraternity. In fact, one picture postcard of the Tübingen Barrel has survived (Figs. 43a–43b), on the back of which the visit to the Giant Barrel is described. In December 1904, a group visit to the castle cellar presumably took place, during which the barrel was viewed "not only from the outside" but also from the inside. The fact that a "girl" was also present, as the young scribe reports when he looked out of the bunghole, reflects the cheerful mood.[68]

Games, fun and legends about the history of the Tübingen Giant Barrel seem to have attracted mainly male visitors. After all, the descent into the dark cellar of the castle with a guide and by means of a lantern or torch—as some post-cards suggest—promised a little adventure. In addition, the prospect to talk about the changing history of the country and the terrifying Duke Ulrich down there together with the castle guide and in front of the barrel was certainly alluring. Maybe even to talk shop: how much wine—converted into litres—could this barrel probably hold? Delightfully getting to the bottom of the question: how many glasses or men were needed to empty such a barrel? And to colourfully imagine: what great a feast would have been possible with such a large wine barrel? To listen to the anecdote of the guide at the end, through which he tried to answer the open question of why the Tübingen Giant Barrel is also called the "large book".

But such and other questions remain purely hypothetical in the light of the empty barrel. Such thoughts evaporate on the way back from the castle cellar to daylight at the latest. But shivers and jokes had been fun! The Tübingen Barrel was and still is worth a visit!—And if you still have any doubts whether it is worth a trip, take a look at the Guinness Book of Records, where it is listed as the oldest of the giant barrels.[69]

Fig. 43a Postcard, Publisher Gebrüder Metz, send 4 Dezember 1911

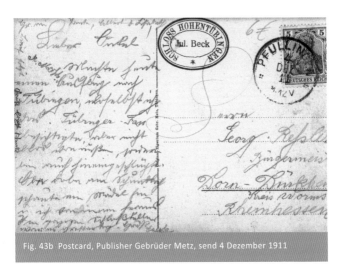
Fig. 43b Postcard, Publisher Gebrüder Metz, send 4 Dezember 1911

COMMENTS WITH LITERATURE

1 Johann Fischart: Affentheurlich Naupengeheurliche Geschicht-klitterung, Straßburg 1582, [p. 112]. http://resolver.staatsbibliothek-berlin.de/SBB0001C2EF00000000 (08.09.2020). Albert Alsleben (ed.): Johann Fischarts Geschichtklitterung (Gargantua). Synoptic impression of the adaptions of 1575, 1582 and 1590, Halle an der Saale 1891, p. 83.

2 Hermann Kurz: Fischart in Tübingen?, in: Germania, New Series Jg. IV., 1871, p. 79–81; Heinrich Hermelink: Die Matrikel der Universität Tübingen, Stuttgart 1906, vol. 1, p. 450, 162. semester of the university (1564), No. 11 „Joannes Piscator Argentoratensis (30. Okt.)"; Ulrich Seelbach: Fischart, Johann, in: Frühe Neuzeit in Deutschland 1520–1620. Literaturwissenschaftliches Verfasserlexikon [VL 16]. Ed. by Wilhelm Kühlmann (among others), vol. 2, Berlin 2012, p. 358–383. "On 30. Oktober 1564, Johannes Piscator Argentoratensis was enrolled in the register of the university of Tübingen, where he can still be found at the end of July 1566." (p. 358).

3 François Desprez: Weibliches Monster im Fass, woodcut, in: Les Songes drolatiques de Pantagruel [...] Rabelais François, Paris 1565. Paris, Bibliothèque nationale de France, département Estampes et photographie, shelf mark: 4-TB-46.

4 Max Eifert: Geschichte und Beschreibung der Stadt Tübingen, Tübingen 1849, p. 130.

5 Friedrich Müller: Württemberg wie es war und ist, Stuttgart 1854, vol. 3, p. 165.

6   Geographisches statistisch-topographisches Lexicon von
    Schwaben, Ulm 1801, vol. 2, p. 852. Beschreibung des Ober-
    amts Tübingen, Stuttgart 1867, p. 216.

7   Hermann Alexander Berlepsch: Chronik vom ehrbaren Bött-
    chergewerk, St. Gallen 1853, p. 105–106. Immanuel Dornfeld:
    Geschichte des Weinbaues in Schwaben, Stuttgart 1868, p.
    144, § 85.

8   Eberhard Werner Happel: Größte Denkwürdigkeiten der Welt
    oder so genannte Relationes curiosae, Hamburg 1685, vol.
    2, p. 194. [Eugen Nägele:] Tübingen und seine Umgebung:
    Ein Führer für Fremde und Einheimische, Tübingen [3]1884, p.
    10–11. Karl Baedeker: Süddeutschland, Leipzig [29]1906, p. 165.

9   Jacob Burckhardt und Wilhelm Lübke: Geschichte der Neueren
    Baukunst, Stuttgart 1872, p. 328.

10 Horace: Odes, 1. Book, 35. Poem "Hymn to Fortuna", lines
    26–27.

11 Josua Eiselein: Die Sprichwörter und Sinnreden des deutschen
    Volkes in alter und neuer Zeit, Freiburg 1840, p. 160.

12 Chalk inscription; above a name: 15[…]3 | R. […] | […]
    Bran[denb]urg | [Mitte drei Namen:] 1563 | J. WS. N. | […] |
    Ober[…] Bar | 1563 | N. O. V | […] Danhau[…] | 1563 | […] | E.
    M. Reax[…] | [three names below:] 1563 | […] Oich | 15[…]3 |
    | […] Wedell | 1563 | […].

13 Hauptstaatsarchiv Stuttgart, shelf mark: A 71 Bü 1194.

14 Inscription on Duke Ulrich's epitaph by Friedrich Kessler from
    1551: "[…] variis fortunae procellis agitatus […]" „driven
    around by manifold storms of fate"). Sebastian Scholz:
    Konfessionelle Aspekte in den Inschriften evangelischer
    Landesherren im 16. Jahrhundert, in: Jürgen Macha et al.
    (ed.): Konfession und Sprache in der Frühen Neuzeit: inter-
    disziplinäre Perspektiven, Münster 2012, p. 177, note. 32. Cf.

also: Stefanie A. Knöll: Die Grabmonumente der Stiftskirche in Tübingen, Stuttgart 2007.

15 Gerhard Raff: Hie gut Wirtemberg alleweg. Das Haus Württemberg von Graf Ulrich dem Stifter bis Herzog Ludwig (Univ. Diss. Tübingen 1984), Stuttgart ⁴1995, p. 457.

16 Expert opinion of the Württemberg councils for Duke Ulrich on his extravagant conduct at court and the state's indebtedness, which could lead to his deposition (Urach, Papier, fol.) [6. Januar 1515], Hauptstaatsarchiv Stuttgart, shelf mark: G 41 Bü2, 1.

17 Karl August Barack (ed.): Zimmerische Chronik, Tübingen 1869, vol. 3, p. 8 [1420]. „Das aber herzog Ulrich in seiner jugendt und auch darnach in seinem alter so abenteurig gewest [...]."

18 Hans Hamburger: Der Staatsbankrott des Herzogtums Wirtemberg nach Herzog Ulrichs Vertreibung und die Reorganisation des Finanzwesens, Schwäbisch Hall 1909.

19 Recently: Götz Adriani, Andreas Schmauder (ed.): 1514 – Macht, Gewalt, Freiheit: der Vertrag zu Tübingen in Zeiten des Umbruchs, Ostfildern 2014, p. 404, No. 171.

20 Cf. the collection of critical tributes to Duke Ulrich, printed in: Raff 1995, p. 458–474. Most recently see: Franz Brendel: Herzog Ulrich von Württemberg, Kaiser Maximilian und der Schwäbische Bund (1487–1519), in: Götz Adriani, Andreas Schmauder (ed.): 1514 – Macht, Gewalt, Freiheit: der Vertrag zu Tübingen in Zeiten des Umbruchs, Ostfildern 2014, p. 282–286.

21 Werner Frasch: Ein Mann Namens Ulrich, Leinfelden-Echterdingen 1991, p. 73.

22 Frasch 1991, p. 257. Vlrich (von gottes gnaden) hertzog zu Wirtemperg vnnd zu Tegke, [enacted on:] 23. April 1515, [Section:] „Item als uß dem zutrincken/trunckenhait", http://

digital.wlb-stuttgart.de/purl/bsz434861251 (08.09.2020). Von Gottes genaden, Wir Vlrich Hertzog zu Wirtemberg, [enacted on:] 16. November 1548, [Section:] „Vom zu Trincken", http://digital.wlb-stuttgart.de/purl/bsz435430149 (06.09.2020).

23 Franz Brendle: Dynastie, Reich und Reformation: die württembergischen Herzöge Ulrich und Christoph, die Habsburger und Frankreich [Tübingen, Univ. Diss., 1997], Stuttgart 1998.

24 Gerd Althoff: Die Macht der Rituale. Symbolik und Herrschaft im Mittelalter, Darmstadt 2003.

25 Götz Adriani, Andreas Schmauder (ed.): 1514 – Macht, Gewalt, Freiheit: der Vertrag zu Tübingen in Zeiten des Umbruchs, Ostfildern 2014. Albert Raff: Herzog Ulrich – schillernder Fürst der deutschen Renaissance, Stuttgart 2009. Werner Frasch: Ein Mann Namens Ulrich, Leinfelden-Echterdingen 1991.

26 Die Chronik der Grafen von Zimmern. Ed. by Hansmartin Decker-Hauff. Darmstadt 1973, vol. 2, p. 184. Der üppige Hof Herzog Ulrichs von Württemberg: „[...] der zeit herzog Ulrich von Würtemberg ein ansehenliche und fürstliche hofhaltung, dergleichen wenig der oberlendischen fürsten, zudem alle ritterspill mit rennen und stechen, auch gemainlich sonst alle adenliche kurzweiln und iebungen mit jagen und andern sachen an solchem hove überflissigclichen gepflegen [...]."

27 Hans-Jürgen Bleyer: Dendrochronologische und gefügekundliche Untersuchung, Tübingen, Schloss-Nordflügel, historisches Fass, 16.02.2018.

28 Hauptstaatsarchiv Stuttgart, shelf mark: A 256 vol. 34; http://www.landesarchiv-bw.de/plink/?f=1-1338075 (06.09.2020). I wish to thank Dr. Regina Keyler for her assistance with the transcription.

29 Letter, 14 Mai 1546, Folio 36r–36v, Hauptstaatsarchiv Stuttgart, shelf mark: A409 Bü 6.

30   Walther Pfeilsticker: Neues württembergisches Dienerbuch, Stuttgart 1957, vol. 1, § 2871: Hans Erhard von Ow, Burgvogt in Tübingen 1530, 1534.

31   Pfeilstricker 1957, vol. 1, § 1764: Kuhn, Landschreiberverwalter ab 1545 bis 1558; § 1657: Kuhn, Kanzleischreiber 1533; § 1664: Kuhn, Landschreiberei-Verwalter 1545 bis 1558.

32   Letter, 4 Oktober, 1546, Folio 38r, Hauptstaatsarchiv Stuttgart, shelf mark: A409 Bü 6.

33   This source for the calculation of the Tübingen Giant Barrel is quoted in: Tübinger Blätter, vol. XIII, 1911, p. 58. „Landschreiberei-Rechnung 1549/50, Blatt 400, folgender Aufschrieb: Maister Symon Bindern Bürgern zu Binigkhaim, bezahlt von dem großen vaß uff Tüwingen, welches XLVII Fuder Weins haltet, zu machen. Lut U G F u. H Beuelch und seiner Quittung also uf der Renntchamer mit ime überkommen, tut 384 fl." Cf. also Theodor Schön: Geschichte von Hohentübingen, Zweiter Teil: Vom Umbau des Schlosses durch Herzog Ulrich bis zur Übergabe an die Kaiserlichen (1534–1634), in: Tübinger Blätter, vol. VIII, 1905, p. 54. Quoted from the manuscript 136 of the royal Geh. Haus- und Staatsarchivs: „Im Keller ligt neben andern ein gar großes vaß. Das hatt gemacht meister Simon, ein kieffer von Binningheim (Bönnigheim) am Necker von anno (15)46 biß anno 1548, hatts zu Binigheim in seinen costen gemacht. Ist hernach Tubingae uffgesetzt worden. Er gab werschaft dazu uff 80, 90 oder 100 jar, vordert, begert dazu zu tauben und böden 40 stamm holtz und zu felgen 50 stamm, die im Rutenhamer (Rutesheim OA. Leonberg) welden gehauen worden. [...] ist das jahr mitt wein gefüllt, helt beheb, cost zu machen 330 gulden und 1 hofclaid. Doch ist das groß vaß zu Haidelberg vil größer, als welches hellt 132 fuder [...]. Kostet das gantze werck ohne das holtz 3166 gulden." The manuscript 136 is today in the Hauptstaatsarchiv Stuttgart, shelf mark: J 1 Nr. 136 I-II; Includes: Bü 1-39 {JOHANN JAKOB

GABELKOVER u.a.: KONZEPT EINER WÜRTTEMBERGISCHEN LANDESBESCHREIBUNG}. Collection of material, alphabetically arranged according to 39 official places, Partial copy Hs 12, 318a–965, a supplement on Blaubeuren Hs 252, 128r–138r, first notes by Oswald Gabelkover LBS Cod. hist. Fol. 22. – preparatory work for O. GABELKOVER, Württ. Geschichte Teil II, s. Hs 3–7a. Enriched with more recent individual descriptions, basis of later land registers (s. Bü 25, 2r is incorporate). 39 single covers, 17th century beginning etc.

34 Copy of [or: from] the miscells and contributions of [Christian Heinrich] Günzler on the history of Württemberg rulers and culture [from 1833 (see Klein, Handschriften Hauptstaatsarchiv, No 103 a-c), by Financial Councillor Rudolf Moser, part of the collection of material describing the Stuttgart city administration], [between 1833 and 1856], p. 11, Staatsarchiv Ludwigsburg, shelf mark: E 258 VI Bü 3642; http://www.landesarchiv-bw.de/plink/?f=2-86176: „Das große Faß auf dem Asperg. | In den älteren Beschreibungen von Heidelberg | wird gemeiniglich auch unter anderen Merk- | würdigkeiten des großen Fasses von Heidel- | berg erwähnt, welches 250 Eimer gehalten | haben soll. Aber auch in Würt. Hofkellerei- | en fanden sich vormals ähnlich große Fässer. | Nach einem vorhandenen schriftlichen Accord| 14. May 1546. übernahm Simon Binder zu | Bönnigheim gegen Herzog Ulrich die Verbindlichkeit | ihm bis zum nächsten Herbst ein großes Faß, wel- | ches 40 Eßlinger Fuder, demnach 240 Eimer | Wein halten soll und wozu der Meister alles | Holz abzugeben hatte, zu verfertigen, welches | Faß auf dem Asperg gebracht und dort in dem | heerschaftl[ichen] Keller aufgesetzt werden mußte. | Neben der Verköstigung während des Aufset- | zens wurden ihm vom Herzog 330 f. [Gulden] bezahlt." I would like to thank Sarah Kupferschmied for her help with the transcription.

35   According to Johannes Kepler's "barrel rule" from 1615, the Tübingen Giant Barrel has a volume of around 84,000 litres. We owe this information to Robert Lutz, Tübingen. Cf.: Christina Häfele und Ernst Seidl: Das Fass und seine Formel, in: Schwäbisches Tagblatt, from 09.01.2019. https://www.tagblatt.de/Nachrichten/Das-Fass-und-seine-Formel-400021.html (08.09.2020).

36   Johann Jakob Gabelkover and others., (folders), Contains: Bü 1-39 (KONZEPT EINER WÜRTTEMBERGISCHEN LANDESBESCHREIBUNG), collection of material, alphabetically according to 39 official places, 39 single covers, early 17th century, Hauptstaatsarchiv Stuttgart, shelf mark: J 1 Nr. 136 II, fol. 13 r; http://www.landesarchiv-bw.de/plink/?f=1-2372915; „Volgt ein Verzaichnus, allerhand fürnemmer, in und an der stadt Türing, fürgenommenen gebaue." [fol. 12 r] Randvermerk: „groß vaß"; „Im Keller ligt neben andern | ein gar großes vaß. Das hatt gemacht M.[eister] Simon, | ein kieffer von Binnigheim [Bönnigheim] am Necker von A°[nno] – [ergänzt von anderer Hand interlinear:] von anno [15]46 biß – 1548, | [ergänzt von anderer Hand am Rand:] hatts zu Binigheim in seinen costen gemacht. Ist hernach Tubingae uffgesetzt worden. Er gab werschaft dazu uff 80, 90 oder 100 jar, vordert, begert dazu zu tauben und böden 40 stämm holtz und zu felgen 50 stämm, die im Rutenhamer [Ruteshaim OA. Leonberg] welden gehauen worden. Meister Mayer, hofbinder allhier, gab sein underthänigstes bedencken, es kend nit über 10 jahr werschafft deß vas sein, weil das holtz erst sol gehauen werden und beid post perfectum opus post biennium in keller kommen, da es stets ligen muß bleiben. Sollt aber circiter 6 oder 7 jahr vor in lufft ligen [Ende der Randnotiz]. Heltt 47 Eßlinger fuder und 4 eimer, ist 24 schuch lang, die bodenhöhe 13 ½ schuch, die sponthöhe 16 ½ schuch, ligt in 14 velgen, ist das jar mitt wein gefüllt, helt beheb, cost zu machen 150 – [durchgestrichen

und von anderer Hand ergänzt:] 330 – gulden | und 1 hofclaid. | Doch ist das groß vaß zu Hai- | delberg vil größer, als welches heltt 132 fuder […]. Kostet | das gantze werck, ohne das holtz 3166 gulden." Vgl. auch zu dieser Quelle: Theodor Schön: Geschichte von Hohentübingen, Zweiter Teil: Vom Umbau des Schlosses durch Herzog Ulrich bis zur Übergabe an die Kaiserlichen (1534–1634), in: Tübinger Blätter, vol. VIII, 1905, p. 54. Dort wird aus der Handschrift 136 des Kgl. Geh. Haus- und Staatsarchivs zitiert, die sich heute im Hauptstaatsarchiv Stuttgart befindet mit der Shelf mark: J 1 Nr. 136 II.

37 Pfeilsticker 1957, vol. 1, § 611. „Mayer, Hofküfer, Georgii 1688."

38 Pfeilsticker 1957, vol. 1, § 606. „Kaiser gen. der Feuerbacher Hans (1567 „Jörg", 1568 „Hans") gewesener Kellerknecht, ist Hofbinder, auch Hofküfer genannt, […]. Er hatte das große Faß gemacht, welches 136 Eimer oder 33 600 Liter faßte und nach dem 2. Weltkrieg noch unversehrt im Keller des Alten Schlosses in Stgt. lag."

39 Brigitte Reinhardt, Stefan Roller (ed.): Michel Erhart & Jörg Syrlin d. Ä., Spätgotik in Ulm, Ulm 2002, p. 36–38.

40 Georg Lill: Hans Fugger (1531–1598) und die Kunst, Leipzig 1908, p. 105, N.B. 1.

41 Max Eifert: Geschichte und Beschreibung der Stadt Tübingen, Tübingen 1849, p. 130. Cf. also: Frasch 1991, p. 265: „Die Kosten für den Festungsbau verschlangen einen großen Teil der herzoglichen Einnahmen. Soweit sich die Ausgaben ermitteln ließen, muß von einem jährlichen Aufwand von vierzigtausend Gulden ausgegangen werden, was etwa einem Drittel der Staatseinnahmen eines Jahres entsprach. An Aufwendungen für den Bau von Landesfestungen und Residenzschlösser […] hat Herzog Ulrich wenigstens fünfhundertsechzigtausend Gulden verbraucht."

42 Rechnungen 1509/10, Hauptstaatsarchiv Stuttgart, Shelf mark
    A 256 vol. 7, fol. 33 v. „Item Wilhelm von Worms platner zu
    Nürnberg bezalt | X von Gl. umb Harnasch durch […]." http://
    www.landesarchiv-bw.de/plink/?f=1-1338048 (08.09.2020).

43 Narcissus Schwelin: Würtembergische kleine Chronica, Oder
    Beschreibung viler denckwürdigen Geschichten […], Stuttgart
    1660, p. 170–171, urn:nbn:de:hbz:061:1-15276 (08.09.2020).

44 The manuscript 136 is today in the Hauptstaatsarchiv Stutt-
    gart, Shelf mark: J 1 Nr. 136 I-II.

45 Ludwig Sturm: Führer durch Tübingen und Umgebung, Tübin-
    gen 1875, p. 12–13.

46 Andreas Christoph Zeller: Ausführliche Merckwürdigkeiten
    der Hochfürstl. Würtembergischen Universitaet und Stadt
    Tübingen […], Tübingen 1743, p. 73. „Er bekame Lohn
    150. fl. und ein Hofkleid." http://mdz-nbn-resolving.de/
    urn:nbn:de:bvb:12-bsb11253360-0 (08.09.2020).

47 Zeller 1743, p. 72.

48 Zeller 1743, p. 73.

49 Württembergische Kirchengeschichte online: https://www·
    wkgo·de/personen/suchedetail?sw=gnd:GNDPFB5484
    (08.09.2020).

50 Johann Ludwig Metz: Tubinga sedes sat congrua musis
    seu dissertatio historico-topographica de Tubinga, oppido
    Wirtembergiae post Stutgardiam metropolin primario /
    Praes.: B. Raith. [Resp.:] Johann Ludwig Metz, Tübingen
    [Univ. Diss.] 1677, p. 10–11, http://mdz-nbn-resolving.de/
    urn:nbn:de:bvb:12-bsb10660079-7 (08.09.2020), „Quam
    tritum & frequentatum hoc ore omnium, tam […] & incertae
    originis est, qualisve vaegrandis ille liber Tubing. & in qua
    asservatus Bibliotheca, Arcisne Ducalis, an Illustr. Collegii, vel
    Biblioth. Universit. Si locus probabili conjecturae est, existi-
    marim ego, ortum esse ex prolixo, poscente ita re, Tractatu

aliquo Theol. haeretico (Pontificius an Calvin. fuerit, parum liquet) opposito, quem urebat pejus, quanto operosius prolixiusque refutatus erat. quid si fuisset spissum illud volumen Confeßionis Würtemberg Illust. Princ. ac DN. DN. CHRISTO-PHORI una cum Apologeticis scriptis. quorum Auth. sunt Johann. Brentius: D. Jacob. Beurlinus: D. Jacob Heerbrand: Dn. Joh. Isenman Abbas in Brentianhausen: D. Theodoricus Schnepsis contra Petr. a Soto? Notum doctis est Graecorum adagium: [...] Callimachus apud Athenaeum lib. 3. sic putat, innuens praestare Laconicam brevitatem, in qua multum sapientiae, Asiaticae laxitati, inqua minus. Multo certius id est, & veritatis exploratioris, grande DOLIUM in Cella Ducal. Arcis reconditum esse. Peregrinis quippe, invisentibus eam, hodieque ostentatur, multaque invisentium jam nomia habet inscripta, adornatum ad mandatum Ducis ULRICI Anno 1548. erogatis Vietori centum thaleris, cujus ambitum atque capacitatem, juxta mensuram Wirtembergico-Esslingensem, computat Narcissus Schwelin. in chronico contractiori Wirtemb. p. 171".

51 Translation of the Latin dissertation of 1677 in extracts see: Matthias A. Deuschle: Brenz als Kontroverstheologe: die Apologie der Confessio Virtembergica und die Auseinandersetzung zwischen Johannes Brenz und Pedro de Soto [Berlin, Diss. Humboldt-Univ., 2005], Tübingen 2006, p. 105.

52 Ludwig Melchior Fischlin: Memoria Theologorum Wirtembergensium Resuscitata: h. e. Biographia Præcipvorvm Virorum, qui à tempore Reformationis usque ad hanc nostram ætatem partim in Ducatu Wirtembergico [...], Ulm 1710, Pars I., p. 321. „[...] Professor Theologus Heidelbergensis, ut in Oratione quandam Inaugurali, d. 11. April. 1616. Habita Sigwartum acerbe admodum & inique traduceret, scriptum ejus vocans hecatomphyllon, centtifolium, das grosse Buch von Tübingen/ plaustrum chartarum & nugarum, Suevica loquentia turgidum, praeter garrulam dicacitatem & Coccysmos, item arguitas

futiles & calumnias multoties protritas, nil quicquam ad rem proferens."

53 Eifert 1848, p. 132–133.

54 The master craftsman Wiedemann and court cooper Ackermann made the barrel by order of Duke Eberhard Ludwig.

55 Th. Cult. Theologiae cultor = student of theology.

56 Johann Benjamin Wolff: Teutschlandes Dreyfaches Denckmahl des Fruchtbahren Weinstockes: Das ist, Gründliche Beschreibung, Der drey Grossen Wein-Fässer in Europa, nebst ausführlicher Relation von der Berg-Vestung Königstein, wie auch Der vornehmsten Städte und Schlösser, des Chur-Fürstenthumbs Sachßen, der Chur-Pfaltz, und des Fürstenthumbs Halberstadt, Magdeburg 1717. http://digital.slub-dresden.de/id375792570 (08.09.2020): Zu Sachsen, „Das Edle I.", p. 65, zur Kurpfalz, die „Geseegnete II.", p. 110, zum Fürstentum Halberstadt, „Das Fruchtbahre III.", p. 151.

57 The barrel of the Königstein fortress in Saxony holds around 250,000 litres, or 249,838 to be precise.

58 Johann Heinrich Zedler: Grosses vollständiges Universal-Lexicon aller Wissenschaften und Künste, Leipzig und Halle 1740, vol. 26, p. 716–717. „Parade, dieses Wort wird denjenigen Sachen beygeleget, die da mehr zum prächtigen Ansehen und zum Staat, als zum Gebrauch dienen sollen, und nur zum Aufputz und Zierde aufgestellt werden, [...]" Johann Christian Wächtlern: Commodes Manual, oder Hand-Buch, darinnen zu finden [...], Leipzig 1714, p. 271. „Parade, die Stellung der Soldaten bey Auff- und Abzug der Wache, auch Ankunft eines Herrns; it. Zierde, Schmuck z.E. dieses Kleid macht eine Parade, es prahlt."

59 Albert Alsleben (ed.): Johann Fischarts Geschichtklitterung (Gargantua). Synoptischer Abdruck der Bearbeitungen von 1575, 1582 und 1590, Halle an der Saale 1891, p. 387. The

term "the big book of Tübingen" can also be found in: Philips van Marnix: Bienenkorb deß Heil. Röm. Immenschwarms, seiner Hummelszellen […], [Straßburg around 1590], Folio 215r; Martin Beer: Gründliche Widerlegung des kurtzen Beweiß Herrn Viti Erbermanni, Nürnberg 1659, p. 476.

60   Georg Braun und Franz Hogenberg: Civitates orbis terrarum, Köln 1588, vol. 4, Tav. 40, a) Eisleben, b) Tubinga [Tübingen]. Cf. also: Alois Schneider u.a.: Tübingen, Stuttgart 2018, p. 166–171 (Series: Archäologischer Stadtkataster Baden-Württemberg, vol. 41.1).

61   In the city description of Tübingen, the "Civitates orbis terrarum" follows older descriptions such as: Sebastian Münster: Cosmographey, oder Beschreibung aller Länder […], Basel 1588, p. dccccxlix. Thübingen. Cap. cccxxvj.

62   Götz Adriani, Andreas Schmauder (ed.): 1514 – Macht, Gewalt, Freiheit: der Vertrag zu Tübingen in Zeiten des Umbruchs, Ostfildern 2014, p. 451, No. 203.

63   Albert Ludwig Grimm: Die malerischen und romantischen Stellen des Neckarthales: in ihrer Vorzeit und Gegenwart, Darmstadt o. J. [around 1832]. Gustav Schwab: Wanderungen durch Schwaben, Leipzig 1837 (Das malerische und romantische Deutschland. In zehn Sektionen: Schwaben, vol. 1). http://archive.thulb.uni-jena.de/hisbest/receive/HisBest_cbu_00025436?&derivate=HisBest_derivate_00011196 (08.09.2020). Cf. Michael Simon, Wolfgang Seidenspinner, Christina Niem (ed.): Episteme der Romantik: Volkskundliche Erkundungen (Mainzer Beiträge zur Kulturanthropologie, Volkskunde, vol. 8), Münster 2014.

64   Eduard Morasch: Das große Faß. Ein Tübinger Fastnachtsschwank aus Herzog Ulrichs Zeit, Tübingen 1899, p. 4; cf. Franz Brümmer: Lexikon der deutschen Dichter und Prosaisten vom Beginn des 19. Jahrhunderts bis zur Gegenwart, vol. 5, Leipzig [6]1913, p. 27.

65 The Tübingen publishing archive with over 300,000 glass plates including rights of use was purchased by the Haus der Geschichte Baden-Württemberg in 1991. https://de.wikipedia.org/wiki/Gebr%C3%BCder_Metz (08.09.2020).

66 Udo Rauch und Antje Zacharias (ed.): … und grüßen Sie mir die Welt. Tübingen – eine Universitätsstadt auf alten Postkarten, Tübingen 2007. In this catalogue the motif of the Giant Barrel is not included.

67 Albrecht Krause: Zu schön, um wahr zu sein. Photographien aus der Sammlung Metz, Stuttgart 1997, p. 40–63.

68 Postcard from 4 December 1911, transcription:„Lieber Onkel! | machte heute | einen Ausflug nach | Tübingen, woselbst ich | das Tübinger Fass | besichtigte, aber nicht | blos von außen, sondern | bin auch hineingeschlüpft. | Eb[e]n dabei am Schundloch [richtiger Begriff: Spundloch] | schaute ein Mädel hin | u.[nd] ich von innen heraus. | Im ganzen Schloßkeller | war es großartig. Gruß Jacob" – "Dear Uncle | made today | a trip to | Tübingen, where I | the Tübingen Barrel | visited, but not | only from the outside but | slipped inside. | just at the bunghole | a girl looked inside| and I from the inside out. | In the whole castle cellar | it was great. Greetings Jacob".

69 https://www.guinnessworldrecords.com/world-records/oldest-wooden-vat (08.09.2020).

FIGURES

The photos were taken by Valentin Marquardt unless otherwise indicated.

Fig. 3: München, Bayerische Staatsbibliothek, Sig. P.o.germ. 375 lb

Fig. 4: Paris, Bibliothèque nationale de France, département Réserve des livres rares, Sign. RES-Y2-2124

Fig. 5: Paris, Bibliothèque Nationale de France, département Estampes et photographie, Sign. 4-TB-46

Fig. 7: Stuttgart, Haus der Geschichte Baden-Württemberg, Sammlung Gebrüder Metz, Inv. 1991/0140/008433

Fig. 9: Gotha, Stiftung Schloss Friedenstein, Schlossmuseum, Graphische Sammlung, inv. no 38, 86, Xyl.I.118

Fig. 11: Kunstsammlung der Fürsten zu Waldburg-Wolfegg, Schloss Wolfegg, inv. no Kasten 69a/B154

Fig. 12: München, Bayerische Staatsgemäldesammlung, Alte Pinakothek, inv. no 2458

Fig. 14: Foto: Edgar Bierende 2019

Fig. 15: Stuttgart, Württembergische Landesbibliothek, Sig. Wirt.R.qt.104

Figs. 16, 17: Hauptstaatsarchiv Stuttgart, Sign. A 256 Bd. 34

Fig. 18: Entnommen aus: Hans Sachs, Eygentliche Beschreibung aller Stände, Frankfurt 1568

Fig. 19: Stuttgart, Württembergische Landesbibliothek, Sign. HBFC 117

Fig. 20: Hauptstaatsarchiv Stuttgart, Sign. J 1 Nr. 136 I-II

Fig. 21: Foto: Kristian Adolfsson 2018

Fig. 22: Photographer unknown, 2013

Fig. 23: Wien, Kunsthistorisches Museum, inv. no Hofjagd- und Rüstkammer, A 237

Fig. 24: Düsseldorf, Universitäts- und Landesbibliothek, Sign. DSPG 319

Fig. 25: Augsburg, Staats- und Stadtbibliothek, Sign. H 2574

Fig. 26: München, Bayerische Staatsbibliothek, Sign. 4 Diss. 633#Beibd.13

Fig. 27: München, Bayerische Staatsbibliothek, VD18 15537587-001

Fig. 28: Dresden, Sächsische Landesbibliothek – Staats- und Universitätsbibliothek, Sign. Hist.Sax.H.1217

Fig. 29: Heidelberg, Universitätsbibliothek, inv. no Graph. Slg. A 0247

Fig. 30: Dresden, Staatliche Kunstsammlung, Kupferstich-Kabinett, inv. no A 133108

Fig. 33: Tübingen, Universitätsbibliothek, Sign. PB 14

Fig. 34: Stuttgart, Staatsgalerie, Graphische Sammlung, inv. no A32209

Fig. 35: Jena, Thüringer Universitäts- und Landesbibliothek, Sign. 4 Itin.VI,5 :2

Fig. 39: Tübingen, Stadtarchiv, Sign. D 150, Album 161, Postkarte 2415

Fig. 42: Tübingen, Stadtarchiv, Sign. D 150, Album 161, Postkarte 2408

Fig. 43a, b: Museum der Universität Tübingen MUT

We have endeavoured to obtain all image rights; should there be, however, unresolved claims in this regard, we are, of course, prepared to comply with them.

ACKNOWLEDGE-
MENTS

Dr. Regina Keyler, Tübinger Universitätsarchiv, Udo Rauch, Stadtarchiv Tübingen, Dr. Peter Schiffer, Hauptstaatsarchiv Stuttgart, and Prof. Dr. Maria Magdalena Rückert, Staatsarchiv Ludwigsburg supported the author in the transcription process and with valuable advice.

Many thanks are also due to Dr. Robert Lutz for calculating the barrel volume according to Johannes Kepler's barrel rule, and to the Stadtverwaltung Tübingen, Fachabteilung Kunst, Kultur und internationale Beziehungen, in particular to Christopher Blum, for obtaining entry into the Guinness Book, and to the former MUT employee Lea Kupferschmied, as well as to the employees at the museum "Alte Kulturen" in Hohentübingen Castle, Christina Häfele and Thomas Klank, for advice and discussions. I would also like to thank my colleagues for the possibility of publishing this volume and for its layout.

ABOUT THE AUTHOR

Dr. Edgar Bierende received his doctorate in 1998 from the University of Basel in the field of art studies with the dissertation "Lucas Cranach the Elder and German Humanism". He began as a research fellow at the Stadtmuseum Düsseldorf, then worked as a research assistant on the exhibition project "Splendour and Ceremonial" in the Munich Residence at the Bavarian Administration of State Palaces, Gardens and Lakes. This was followed by a period as an assistant at the University of Bern. From 2011 onwards, he coordinated the digital cataloguing project for the portrait collections of the University of Tübingen. Dr. Edgar Bierende has been working as collection coordinator at the Museum of the University of Tübingen MUT since 2013. In this context, he has published among others fundamental articles on the medical moulage collections and the mathematical model collection and is currently working on a publication on the palaeontological display collection of the University of Tübingen.

SPONSORS

Erika-Völter-Stiftung
Tübingen

Universitätsbund
Tübingen e. V.

Kreissparkasse
Tübingen

Credits

Brief Monographs by MUT
Published by Ernst Seidl und Michael La Corte

Volume 14

Edgar Bierende:
The Oldest Giant Wine Barrel.
A Superlative at Hohentübingen Castle

Translation: Hannah Herrera, Ella Ujhelyi
Editorial: David Kühner, Michael La Corte, Ernst Seidl
Layout: Michael La Corte, Adna Valjevac
Print: Gulde Druck, Tübingen

EBERHARD KARLS
UNIVERSITÄT
TÜBINGEN

MUSEUM DER
UNIVERSITÄT
MUT

ISBN: 978-3-9821339-5-9

BRIEF MONOGRAPHS

Volume 1, Ingrid Gamer-Wallert: Die Tübinger Mastaba, 2014
Volume 2, Kathrin B. Zimmer: Der Tübinger Waffenläufer, 2015
Volume 3, Thomas Beck: Schlosslabor Tübingen, 2015
Volume 4, Thomas Beck: The Tübingen Castle Laboratory, 2015
Volume 5, Nicholas Conard: Das Vogelherdpferd, 2016
Volume 6, Nicholas Conard: The Vogelherd Horse, 2016
Volume 7, Volker Harms: Das Tübinger Poupou, 2017
Volume 8, Volker Harms: The Tübingen Poupou, 2017
Volume 9, Jürgen Kost: Die Tübinger Schlosssternwarte, 2018
Volume 10, Jürgen Kost: The Castle Observatory in Tübingen, 2020
Volume 11, Ingrid Gamer-Wallert: The Mastaba of Tübingen, 2019
Volume 12, Kathrin B. Zimmer: The Tübingen Hoplite, 2020
Volume 13, Edgar Bierende: Das älteste Riesenweinfass, 2020
Volume 14, Edgar Bierende: The Oldest Giant Wine Barrel, 2020

Octavo format, round about 100 pages, 4,90 Euros
https://www.unimuseum.uni-tuebingen.de/de/shop.html